# WILLIAM HARTLEY

## THE GREATEST NAME IN JAM-MAKING

*"We have great competition and the house that makes the best article at the most reasonable price should win. I want us to be that house."* William Hartley meant it when he said those words. During his lifetime he established Hartley's as the leading brand of jam in the UK, a position it still proudly holds today. Hartley's products are also sold across the world.

In achieving his phenomenal success William Hartley was not driven by selfish ambition. The purpose of his life, he said, was to *"serve the Lord every day to the best of my ability"*. His greatest joy was using his immense wealth to enrich the lives of others.

### Growing up in Colne

William Pickles Hartley (Pickles was his mother's maiden name) was born in Colne, Lancashire, on the edge of the Pennines. It was principally a cotton-weaving town when William was born there on 23 February 1846. His father, John, was a tinsmith and a local Methodist preacher. His mother, Margaret, ran a small grocery shop in Colne. Sadly, William was the only one of their children to survive infancy.

**Above:** *Colne, Lancashire*

He was immensely grateful for his Christian upbringing and stated:

*"My parents and grandparents were godly people. I was always under the deepest religious impressions."*

He also gratefully acknowledged the influence of his chapel Sunday School teacher whose character and deep spirituality made a lasting impression on him. As a result of these influences William declared, *"I never remember a time when I had not an earnest desire to be good."*

The Hartley family were members of the Primitive Methodist Church, a branch of Methodism that aimed to be as close as possible to the denomination's earliest roots, thus 'primitive' meaning 'original'. For many years he was the chapel's organist which also involved training the choir. Additionally, he served as a Sunday School teacher and as the chapel's treasurer.

At the time William was growing up it was quite normal for children as young as eight to work six and a half hours a day six days a week in the cotton mills. However, John and Margaret denied themselves the extra income William could have brought into the home had they sent him out to work. Instead, they enrolled him at a local school founded by a voluntary organisation for the education of working-class children. At 13 he transferred to Colne Grammar School.

## First steps in business

On leaving the grammar school at 14, William worked in his mother's grocery shop. It was here that he discovered an appetite for commerce. After two years in the shop he became frustrated that the business could not grow in its small, cramped premises. When he heard that a much larger shop was available in Colne's main street he tried to persuade Margaret to take it and allow him to run it. She flatly refused, dismissing his idea as *"headstrong rashness"*. It worried her that her son was capable of such foolish thinking.

However, a fellow chapel member, whose opinion Margaret respected, managed to convince her that William's idea was actually very sensible. In the end she bought the shop and put William in charge of it. And so, at 16, he became a businessman. And it quickly became obvious that he was a very good one.

*Above: William's mother, Margaret*

At a time when there was no proper refrigeration

4

he saw the need for a saltery, somewhere for people to buy ready salted food or have their own food salted to prolong its life. He therefore added this facility to his grocery business. He also saw further opportunity for growth by offering local retailers a wholesale service, selling them grocery items in bulk.

In developing the wholesale side of his business, William walked long distances across the moors to collect orders or make deliveries and often had to set off from home at five in the morning to get to his first customer by seven. Years later he recalled how tough it was:

> *"I walked to Haworth, Oakworth and to Keighley Station, so tired that I was very glad to sit down in the station. I walked about twenty miles, I had called on twenty customers, and on many a journey I did not make a shilling. It took a good deal of resolution to keep that up."*

His *"resolution to keep that up"* combined with his customers' trust in the reliability of his products won him an ever growing clientèle. He never mixed dubious ingredients into his items unlike some of his unscrupulous competitors after an easy profit. There was no brick dust in his cocoa or ground rice in his sugar. And his weights and measures were always accurate. Dishonest practice had been commonplace until the passing of the Adulteration of Food, Drink

*Above: William, aged 19*

5

and Drugs Act in 1872 and against this background William's integrity stood out. As a result his business flourished.

### Marriage

In May 1866, with the security of his thriving business behind him, William, aged 20, married Martha Horsfield his childhood sweetheart, now 23. Martha was the daughter of a Colne grocer and the youngest of 13 children, a sharp contrast to William growing up as an only child.

Their honeymoon was quite extraordinary seen through today's eyes. William gives us an account:

*"We were married on a Whit-Monday morning ... Holidays were then a very rare thing in our native town of Colne. Indeed, we scarcely knew what the word 'holiday' was in the language. However, we were quite as happy with half a day on that Whit-Monday as we have been since with a month's holiday. On that afternoon we spent our honeymoon in processioning [through] the town of Colne with the Sunday School scholars and singing the special Whitsuntide hymns in the principal streets of our native town; and I was at business as usual next morning as though nothing had happened."*

Their marriage was to be a long and happy one. They were to have eight daughters and a son. Martha proved to be the perfect wife for William. Like him, she had a deep Christian faith and she supported him wholeheartedly in all his church and philanthropic activities. She had a sharp mind and an instant grasp of business. She became a familiar figure at his works and frequently gave him wise and welcome advice in business matters.

### The jam manufacturer is born

By the time he was 25, William's business had grown to become one of the largest wholesale operations in Lancashire. Despite the demands on his time, he never allowed his church activities to suffer. As he explained:

> *"In those early days I paid the closest attention to my business, but on Sundays I always devoted the whole day to work in connexion with the chapel. ... my Sunday duty was: Sunday School 9 o'clock, service at 10.30, school at 1.15, afternoon service at 2.30, evening service at 6, prayer meeting at 7.30, and occasionally an open-air mission at 5.30 previous to the evening service."*

But in an unexpected twist of circumstances, the nature and direction of his business changed. His jam supplier had become unreliable so William stopped doing business with him. But this left him in a difficult position – there was no other source of supply. Not wanting to disappoint his customers, he made a life-changing decision: he would make jam himself. And so, in the summer of 1871, with a workforce of 12, he produced his first 100 tons.

From the outset he was determined that only the best quality would do. As with the contents of other products he sold, his jam would contain no dubious ingredients. There would be no turnips to boost the weight, no carrots as a substitute for sugar, no tiny chips of wood to look like seeds. He scrutinised the entire manufacturing process to ensure the purity and cleanliness of his product.

William's jam was an instant success and the price was reasonable. Sales went from strength to strength. Within three years the demand so greatly exceeded supply that he decided to give up the wholesale business and concentrate solely on jam-making. But was Colne the right place to do this, he wondered?

### Re-location to Bootle
There were compelling reasons to stay in Colne. He loved his home town, his business was thriving, he had a settled family life with Martha and his four daughters and he was happy in his chapel. But it made no sense to build a larger factory there. He needed to be more strategically placed on the railway network for distribution purposes, nearer to the Liverpool sugar refineries to reduce transportation costs of sugar to his works, nearer to the Mersey docks to reduce transportation costs to his works of oranges for marmalade production

*Above:* The Mersey docks

**Above:** *The Leeds-Liverpool Canal at Bootle*

and close to fruit-growing farms. After weighing up all the options, he found that Bootle ticked all these boxes. He felt strongly that he should relocate there.

He told family and friends what he had in mind but was wholly unprepared for their reaction. *"There was no exception to the adverse criticism."*, he said. Everyone accused him of *"vaulting ambition"*. Why wasn't he satisfied with what he had? They warned him that he was tempting fate by being so greedy and predicted disaster.

Their comments hurt him very deeply. He wrote later that he *"never felt so alone"*. But despite total lack of support, he was convinced he had to go. And so he sold his wholesale business in Colne and in June 1874 opened a factory in Pine Grove, Bootle, next to the Leeds-Liverpool Canal.

## Early struggles in Bootle

William and Martha left Colne with their four daughters and moved into 12 Park Street close to the factory. Things soon started to go wrong. Within a year they tragically lost their youngest daughter, also called Martha, aged just 19 months. And in the business sphere there were crushing pressures.

William had invested all his available capital in the construction of the new works and needed a loan to buy fruit and sugar. But it was difficult to find a lender. The first offer he received was on the condition that the lender be made a partner but Martha persuaded William against this. The only loan he could get was over seven years at an exorbitant rate which swallowed 75% of his profits. As a result, money was extremely tight, both at home and in the business. William was continually burdened by financial worries and worked long hours to try to make ends meet. *"For

**Above:** *William and his family*

*a number of years in our early days we had great difficulties and our first struggles were severe indeed.",* he recalled.

## The joy of giving

The pressures on William in no way deflected him from his commitment to the Bootle Primitive Methodist Chapel where the family worshipped. He served faithfully as the organist, playing at every service and spending considerable time training the choir.

In the midst of their severe financial difficulties William and Martha made an incredible decision that seemed to defy all logic. It was a decision that revealed the depth of their Christian faith. William tells the story:

> *"Probably the greatest event of my life occurred on January 1, 1877. On that day my wife and I made a written vow that we would devote a definite and well-considered share of our income for religious and humanitarian work, and that this should be a first charge, and that we should not give to the Lord something when we had finished with everything else."*

They decided, whatever their personal needs, to give 10% of their gross income to *"the needs of mankind."* What moved them to do this? As William once wrote to a friend: *"When we think of the life and sacrifice of Jesus Christ, then nothing we can do is too much."*

The realization that he could use money to make a significant difference to the lives of others was a liberating experience for William. He said that it marked the beginning of *"The real, deep, lasting, and genuine happiness of my own Christian life"*. He and Martha resolved that the percentage they would give should increase in proportion to the growth of their income, and even if their circumstances took a dramatic downturn, they would never give less than 10%. In fact, their giving over the years continually increased, eventually reaching 30% of gross income.

William asked God to show him where the money should be placed. He did not want to give randomly or impulsively:

*"My daily prayer is that God will show me what He wishes me to do. I only want to see clearly His guiding hand, and I am daily asking Him to lead me".*

He admitted it was not easy at first to carry out this resolve. He was shocked to find that his natural instinct as an entrepreneur was to make money, not give it away. He described his inner conflict in the following way:

*"The lower self at once asserted its claim, and said, 'I have it, and it is mine.' But the higher self, if it was in full sympathy with the teaching of Jesus Christ, would rise above the temptation and be ready in some reasonable degree to share with others."*

As he began to form the habit of giving, William became aware that his selfish impulses gradually weakened. Eventually he was able to say:

*"The more we cultivate the spirit of Jesus Christ, the*

*easier the thing becomes, and what appeared to us quite impossible at the beginning becomes not only possible but absolutely a joy."*

During his times of struggle William never lost sight of his obligation to his customers. He maintained the highest standards of production and kept his prices at very reasonable levels. He declared:

*"Our aim has always been to win the confidence of the public by making the best possible article and selling it at a fair price, and on that principle our business has gone from strength to strength."*

Such was the reputation of Hartley's jam that demand soared and an extension to the factory had to be built. Then another. The growth of the business was unstoppable. Despite the punitive nature of the loan, William was in a position to repay the outstanding balance well before the seven years of the loan were up. But the lender refused. The interest payments were much too attractive.

*Above: Enjoying Hartley's jam*

### Challenge offers

As he had vowed, William unhesitatingly shared his good fortune with others. He frequently donated enormous sums of money unconditionally but sometimes, to discourage an over-reliance on handouts, he adopted the principle of 'challenge offers'. He wanted people to experience, as he had done, *"the luxury of doing good"*. He would donate a specified amount towards a stated target on condition that the balance was found by the collective efforts of others.

When he learned in 1884 that the Primitive Methodist Missionary Society was in deep financial trouble, he immediately offered to help. The Society had accumulated a debt of £5,000 – a massive amount at the time – and did not have the resources to pay it. In accordance with his principle of challenge offers William offered to pay £1,000 of the Society's debt if the balance of £4,000 could be raised. This had exactly the effect he wanted. It appealed to people's imagination and they rose to the challenge. Within a year £4,542 was raised and the debt cleared. William eventually became treasurer of the Missionary Society and regularly gave it generous financial support.

**Re-location to Aintree**
In 1885, after 11 years of continual growth, William's business was incorporated as William Hartley & Sons Ltd. By this time no further growth in Bootle was possible as all available space for extension had been exhausted. Once again William decided to re-locate.

But this time he was not tormented by accusations of *"vaulting ambition"* and gloomy predictions of disaster. Remembering the pain these had caused him – and reflecting on the success he had achieved in Bootle – he urged caution on those who were too easily prepared to pass judgement. Without intending in the slightest to

be triumphalist (William never bore grudges), he openly stated:

> *"Whenever I look back upon that stirring period of my life, I often think how careful we should be in forming adverse views as to the conduct of others for fear that our criticism should prove to be wrong. It was so in my case."*

He found an ideal site for a new factory at the junction of two major railway lines and within easy reach of the Liverpool docks. It was in open countryside about three miles to the east of Bootle close to the village of Aintree, home of the famous Grand National steeplechase. Opening in 1886, the factory became one of the largest of its kind in the world producing 600 tons of jam a week, enough to fill 1.3 million one pound earthenware pots. About a quarter of the world's Seville oranges were shipped here.

William had a permanent workforce of 800 which rose to 2,000 in the busy summer season when the fruit was harvested. He could easily have employed a steady number of employees throughout the year but, unlike other jam manufacturers who pulped their fruit and added preservatives to maintain a

*Above: A picking room, Aintree factory*

constant monthly rate of production, he made his jam as soon as the fruit arrived in the factory. This led to the confident claim *"Fruit gathered at sunrise is Hartley's Jam the same evening."*

To maintain the quality and the distinctive taste of his jam, William personally sampled each boiling and inspected up to a thousand jars at a time. He wanted nothing but the best for his customers. In fact, the company's trademark was a lighthouse, a Christian symbol associated with trust and safety. He wanted his customers to know his products were trustworthy.

But maintaining standards was a constant challenge. For one thing, the unreliability of the weather caused many problems. Too little sunshine caused a slower rate of ripening which delayed the start of the production process. Late frost or too much rain led to a reduced crop, while too large a crop resulted in wastage because much of it would deteriorate faster than it could be processed. Suppliers were another problem. They were often unreliable, sometimes delivering fruit late or delivering fruit that was either too small, not fully ripe or over-ripe.

The stress of these problems, combined with the day-to-day demands of running the company, often exhausted William. At times it affected his health and, despite his naturally cheerful temperament, sometimes made him depressed. He repeatedly ignored advice to slow down. He did, however, refuse to open a factory in the USA, despite good sales to that market. He knew he couldn't spread himself thinly enough to control quality both at home and in the States.

### "My people"

Whatever the pressures on himself, William ensured they were not passed on to his workers. In the treatment of his employees, he said that he always tried *"to carry out the teaching of Jesus Christ"*. He referred to them as *"my people"* and knew each one by name. He enjoyed *"the happiest relations"* with them.

Their working conditions mattered to him. The factory was well ventilated, and wholesome, well-prepared food was sold in the dining hall at cost price. If he noticed a task was physically too demanding, he would ask:

*Above: Aintree factory dining hall*

17

*"What can be done to take the hardness out of this job? Never mind the cost."*

When he discovered that he personally wasn't able to push a truck in a newly delivered batch, he ordered, *"Scrap them!"*

As women outnumbered men by four to one, he looked for every possible means of making their work light and safe. He had all the tram lines in the factory laid out in very gentle gradients to make it easier for them to push loaded trucks. He also had sunken floor areas built for them to stand in so that they could fill pots with jam at a comfortable level with the work surfaces. This would save them having to bend.

He provided free medical care, employing the full-time services of a doctor and nurse. He also established a pension fund which he wholly financed himself. No contributions were ever asked from the workforce. The fund provided a means of income for any employee who had reached retirement age or could no longer work because of accident or illness. One year he took

*Right: Sunken floor areas, Aintree factory*

every employee over the age of eighteen on a five-day visit to Scotland. He paid not only all hotel and travel costs but also everyone's full wages for the duration of the trip.

## Hartley's Village

In 1888, two years after the factory had opened, William built a garden village alongside it to create a pleasant and healthy living environment for his employees. It became known as Hartley's Village. It had an ornamental lake and a bowling green and close by was a sports field. The streets were tree-lined and named after ingredients used in jam-making such as Sugar Street, Spice Street, Plum Street and Cherry Row. Each house had a front garden and running water, a luxury at the time. In spite of the superior quality of these homes, William deliberately kept the rents *"exceedingly low"* as he did not want to make a profit from them.

*Above:* Spice Street, Hartley's Village

*Below:* Cherry Row, Hartley's Village

Shortly afterwards he built a Primitive Methodist chapel nearby for his employees. He and his family worshipped there themselves when they later moved close to the factory. Two of his daughters were married there.

*Right:* Aintree Primitive Methodist Chapel

*Below:* A delivery of oranges, Aintree factory

## Profit-sharing

William believed he had a moral obligation to share his wealth with those who helped create it. He considered his employees equal partners in a shared enterprise and told them:

*"Our interests are mutual. I cannot carry on the business without your co-operation and I venture to think that in my capacity as your employer I render some service to you."*

In 1889 he introduced an annual profit-sharing scheme. He distributed the profits according to individual performance and spent long periods familiarising himself with each person's work. He stressed he was not there to judge but to encourage:

W. P. HARTLEY'S AINTREE WORKS

THIS is Sugar Street—a covered roadway in Hartley's works. During the year about 15,000 tons of sugar are unloaded for the making of Hartley's Jams and Marmalade. The view shows some loads of Seville Oranges just arrived from the steamer

*"I must be in personal touch with practically every one of my workpeople and I am sure it works well. They all feel that they are not lost in the size of the business but are in direct contact with me, and they like this ... There is nothing like it for cementing good feeling between employer and employed."*

Other manufacturers were intrigued by the scheme, assuming there must be some commercial benefit in it. They wanted to know more. William explained to them:

*"Profit-sharing is over and above a fair and just wage, and is given, not because I think it pays commercially ... but because it seems to me right, and doing as I would be done by."*

The enquirers immediately lost interest.

The annual distribution of profits was a special social occasion with music. It was as happy for William as it was for his employees. He told them:

*"Whatever pleasure it gives you to receive the profit-sharing, I can say with perfect sincerity that it gives me equal pleasure to hand it to you."*

## "Doing as I would be done by"

There were other ways in which William put into practice the principle of *"doing as I would be done by."* One was to ensure that his employees always received a fair wage. He publicly declared that if anyone in any department of the works could show that they were paid less than the workers in rival companies, he would increase their wages immediately. In fact, his wages were already higher than those of his competitors. From time to time he actually increased the wages of all his employees without being asked. No-one ever complained about their earnings.

William would sometimes show his appreciation for good work in the most unexpected way. On one occasion, when a boiler had been built in record time, he asked the man concerned to come and see him. On the table in William's office were several piles of gold coins, each pile worth £50 (about £6,000 today). When the man came in, William placed one of the piles in an envelope, handed it over to him and quietly left before the man could thank him.

*Above: Checking oranges for quality, Aintree factory*

He encouraged any employee in financial trouble to come to him for help and established a Benevolent Fund for this purpose. He was always very sympathetic to cases of genuine distress but he made it clear that debts incurred as a result of drink or gambling would meet with no sympathy.

### The split at Everton Football Club
William's keen social conscience and willingness to help others

involved him in many public causes. One to which he was deeply committed was temperance, the fight against alcohol and the misery it caused. He supported a number of local organisations dedicated to this aim and was active nationally as Vice-president of the British Temperance League. He was also a staunch member of the Liberal Party which supported the temperance cause. Through these channels he came to know members of the management committee of Everton Football Club in Liverpool. When a serious crisis arose at the club in 1891 he became involved in it.

The trigger was a clash with Everton's president, John Houlding, over financial matters. Houlding owned the club's ground in the Anfield district and when he wanted to increase the rent for its use there was fierce opposition. There was also fierce opposition to his proposal that the club should buy his ground and be incorporated as a company. The committee considered his asking price to be exorbitant.

*Above:* John Houlding, President, Everton FC

But opposition to Houlding operated at a much deeper level. He was a brewer and one of his public houses, the Sandon, was Everton's HQ. This was wholly incompatible with the strong temperance climate within the club and it extended into the political sphere. Houlding was a prominent member of the Conservative Party which looked after the interests of brewers. Most members of the Everton management committee, on the other hand, were active members of the temperance-supporting Liberal Party. William, as a Liberal councillor on

Liverpool City Council, was well aware of the tension this caused within the club.

The serious clash of values with his committee finally led Houlding to expel them from Anfield in 1892 and continue Everton Football Club there without them. But one of his most outspoken opponents on the committee, George Mahon, appealed to the Football Association (the game's ruling body) claiming that Houlding had no legal right to the name 'Everton'. The appeal was upheld. Houlding

was informed he could continue to run a club at Anfield but under a different name. He chose Liverpool.  A famous local rivalry was born.

Anticipating expulsion from Anfield, Mahon had already found a site on which to construct a new stadium about a mile away across Stanley Park. But there was a serious shortfall of capital. If it was not found the stadium

*Above:* George Mahon, Houlding's fierce opponent

24

*Left:* Anfield Stadium, Liverpool FC

*Below:* Goodison Park, Everton FC

could not be built and without a ground the club would lose its place in the Football League and probably go out of existence.

William and a number of others came to the rescue, forming a consortium pledged to supply the crucial shortfall as an interest-free loan without expectation of return if things went wrong. There were loud cheers when his was the first of the sponsors' names to be read out at a large public gathering. He was one of two people who pledged the largest single amount.

The new stadium, named Goodison Park after the road in which it stood, was opened on 24 August 1892 amidst great fanfare. The club's continued existence and its place in the Football League were now secured. For his part in making this possible, William is still heralded today as one of the saviours of Everton Football Club.

### Aintree Institute and the Beatles

It was William's commitment to the temperance cause

**Above:** *Aintree Institute, Liverpool*

that drew him into the dispute at Everton. His commitment to this cause was evident in other ways, too. Determined to do what he could to provide a counter-attraction to drink, he conceived the idea of a well-equipped community and recreation centre to be built near his works. He had in mind a building with a concert hall accommodating 650 people, a gymnasium, billiard rooms, classrooms, a lecture-room and dining rooms. It would be surrounded by bowling greens and tennis courts.

He wanted this centre to be much more than a private initiative. He was keen to foster a spirit of co- operation in humanitarian work between churches across denominational divides. His dream was of a centre *"for everything that was elevating and of a Christlike character"* run by an inter- denominational committee. He put the idea to a meeting of church representatives in March 1892 and offered £1,000 (£125,000 today) to get the project going.

But the idea was rejected. For another two and a half years he tried to win support for it but met with no enthusiasm. He finally admitted that if the centre was to be built, he would have to fund it alone. Disappointed but undeterred, he saw the project through. The Aintree Institute was opened on 3 November 1896.

It ran successfully as a recreation centre for well over a century.

It has a close association with the Beatles. Prior to the release of their first record, they played there 52 times.

### Queen Victoria's Diamond Jubilee

Another cause close to William's heart was the fight against sickness and disease. He gave vast amounts of money for the construction of hospitals, the endowment of beds and for medical research. He financed cancer research at Liverpool University and also supported the University's School of Tropical Medicine, not least because of its benefits for missionary work. His generous giving extended far and wide but he never forgot the needs of his home town, Colne.

Although he had left Colne for business reasons, his affection for the town remained deep and lasting. He kept up-to-date with its affairs by subscribing to the local newspaper and it thrilled him to meet old friends there: *"It's like meat and drink to me to see those people."*

Reading the Colne newspaper one day in 1897, he noticed a report of a meeting considering how to commemorate Queen Victoria's Diamond Jubilee. He immediately wrote to the Mayor with a proposal – *"I am willing to provide the money to build and furnish a Cottage Hospital for Colne"*.

But he made a condition intended to stimulate others to give, too:

*"that the people of Colne and neighbourhood subscribe a similar amount for an endowment fund."*

*Above: Cottage Hospital, Colne*

In other words, he would build the hospital but – at a time when there was no National Health Service – the public must be willing to pay for its running.

William's condition was accepted and planning went ahead. At the Mayor's invitation, he laid the foundation stone of the hospital on 1 April 1899. In his address, William referred to the responsibility of wealthy people such as himself to help others:

*"The teaching of Jesus Christ was that those who ... turned up at the top, owed a great debt, and by a portion of their money, knowledge and time, they should redeem this debt for the benefit of those who were less endowed."*

The Colne Cottage Hospital was completed within 12 months and opened 20 April 1900.

### Pleas for help

As a public benefactor known for his generosity, William received countless pleas for help. He gave each one personal and prayerful consideration, knowing he needed to exercise wisdom and sensitivity in the distribution of *"the Lord's money"* as he called it. He considered himself merely the steward, not the owner of the money he made.

He was always conscious that financial help given to one might easily be at the expense of another deserving case of need. Of course, the careful examination of requests for help was a time-consuming process but William considered it necessary if he was to make the right decisions. He also felt that merely giving money was not, in itself, enough. He believed he should also become actively involved with causes he financed by attending relevant meetings and events. Again, this made great demands on his time but he gave it willingly.

He also gave anonymously and had a network of trusted friends whose task it was to inform him of cases of dire need. He never questioned his friends' judgement; he only ever asked if the amount they recommended was actually enough.

### New factory in London

William's generosity was accompanied by the continual growth of his business. Sales of his jam had been booming in the North and Midlands but gradually Southerners who had holidayed in the North had become aware of it and began to look for it back home. Furthermore, established customers moving south were keen to continue buying it. Demand in the South became so great that William decided to start production in London with the help of his son John.

He found a suitable site in Green Walk, Bermondsey, and built a new factory on it. When finished, it was one of the capital's largest. It was formally opened on 25 June 1901. At the opening ceremony William proudly told reporters:

*"The supreme object will be to turn out the purest and best article which the most advanced science and art of preserve-making can command. Hartley's makes only one quality – the best."*

It was a claim he lived up to. He took the greatest care in the selection of fruit and ensured it was cleaned with specialist machines on arrival at the factory. Three doctors who inspected the manufacturing process gave the following glowing report:

*"We are exceedingly well pleased with the entire arrangements. The fruit was most excellent; its condition*

**HARTLEY'S JAM PRESERVES AND TABLE JELLIES**
Aerial View of London Works.

LONDON WORKS

*Above: London Works*

*could not have been better, and everything used in the manufacture of the jam was all that we could desire."*

As the reputation of Hartley's jam continued to spread in the South, the works had to be enlarged twice to keep up with demand. Such was the volume of business that there was a constant shuttle of deliveries along Tower Bridge Road between the factory and its own private wharf on the Thames.

Incredibly, William made little use of advertising in achieving his success. When a new salesman wrote to him asking for a sample of the company's products to display, William confidently replied:

*"Dear Sir, The name is the sample."*

This was not arrogance. It was an accepted fact that Hartley's did indeed make *"the best".*

### Supporting medical research

In 1901, the same year that his London factory was opened, William saw work commence on new botanical laboratories he had funded at Liverpool University. The Botany Department had previously been housed in inadequate accommodation in old buildings. William valued the Department's research into the medicinal properties of plants and was delighted to provide fully equipped laboratories in a purpose-built centre to facilitate work of such importance.

The centre was opened on 10 May 1902 and named the Hartley Botanical Institute in his honour. In an expression of gratitude to

William at the ceremony, he was thanked not only for his generosity in funding the Institute but also *"for the personal interest he has shown in the details of its arrangement and equipment."*

In reply William explained how uplifting it was to be involved with organisations like the Botanical Institute. He told the audience that he found it liberating, as a businessman, to have *"an outlet from the commercial into the distinctively Christian atmosphere"*.

He expanded this point on a later occasion when presenting workshops for the blind in Liverpool:

*"A successful businessman needed some corrective, some safety valve, some definite means of escape into the larger life of the higher world."*.

At the same time he stressed that generosity is not measured by what people gave but by what they had left. He had a very keen sense of perspective.

### Hartley College, Manchester

Another of William's interests was education. He was a member of the Walton School Board during his time as a Liverpool councillor and made regular contributions towards the cost of lessons about the dangers of alcohol. He was also a major benefactor of the Primitive Methodists' theological college in Manchester where the denomination's ministers were trained. William twice funded major extensions to it, making it one of the largest theological colleges in Britain.

As Vice-president of the British and Foreign Bible Society William attached great importance to the teachings of the Bible. He wanted Primitive Methodist ministers to be so thoroughly grounded in Biblical knowledge and understanding that they could provide quality teaching for their congregations. He felt that the current training period of two years was too short to ensure the proper standard was reached and tried to persuade the college authorities to extend it to three. Aware that such a move would involve an increase in student numbers and additional pressures on residential accommodation, he offered to provide the necessary funding.

At first there was no general agreement that extended training was necessary and so plans for development did not go ahead. Eventually, however, the wisdom of William's recommendation was realised and his offer of financial support accepted. The required accommodation was duly built.

*Above:* Hartley College, Manchester

Within a few years the demand for Primitive Methodist ministers had grown to such an extent that a further extension was necessary. Once again, William provided the funding. This made possible the building of new staff and student accommodation, improved lecture facilities, a new library and a college chapel.

These facilities were opened on 18 June 1906 and, in gratitude to William, the college was renamed Hartley College.

## A knighthood

William's generosity extended to many more organisations and institutions than those already mentioned. By 1908 he was recognized as one of the country's leading philanthropists and was knighted by King Edward VII on 21 July that year *"in recognition of the many princely acts of beneficence and philanthropy rendered by Sir William to his country."*

Colne was particularly proud of him – he was the first person from his home town to receive this honour.

## Freedom of Colne

A year after receiving his knighthood, William was also honoured in his home town. At a meeting on 28 July 1909, the Mayor of Colne read out a resolution by the Town Council placing on record

> *"its appreciation of the high esteem in which Sir William Hartley of Aintree is held by the inhabitants of his native town; and in recognition of the many valuable services rendered by Sir William to the Borough, as well as to the community at large, that he should be created a Freeman of the Borough."*

He went on to say, *"I am proud that we, in Colne, can claim such a gentleman as a native."*

At the Mayor's Banquet at Colne Town Hall on 9 November William was formally presented with the award. In his reply he explained how much it meant to him:

*Above: Colne Town Hall*

*"The honour of being a Freeman of Colne touches me very much … The ups and downs of life and the development of a business career often take men from the home of their childhood. That has been so in my case. But there are few men who do not retain happy memories of the playground of their youth and the place where their ambitions were born."*

At the ceremony, appreciation was expressed to William for his gift of the Cottage Hospital and of the Hartley Homes. William responded by touching on a theme close to his heart:

*"I am very proud of my native town. If I am to judge from my own experience, the pleasure of memory is much enhanced when, after the lapse of years, one desires to share with his native town those fruits of prosperity which may be made helpful to the many who in the fulness of life are less happily circumstanced. It is … the first duty of those who have money to remember in a liberal manner those who have not … Where much is given much is required."*

## Hartley Homes, Colne

The homes for the aged poor referred to above were opened two years later. They were built as a complex of twenty almshouses on a site with marvellous countryside views and surrounded by beautiful grounds. William not only paid for the houses to be built but also provided money for their upkeep and for the services of a gardener.

At the opening ceremony, he spoke fondly of his and Martha's association with Colne:

> *"Lady Hartley and I are to-day on familiar ground. We were both born in Colne. We passed our early days here. We were both under the influence of good parents and teachers here, especially at Sunday School, whose wise counsel had a lasting effect upon us. Although we left Colne about thirty-eight years ago, we have never forgotten the helpful influences that surrounded us in our early days."*

At a time when women did not have the right to vote, he made a statement at the ceremony about the management of the homes that would have surprised, even shocked, many:

> *"My present idea is that one third of the management committee should be women. I dare say in a short time there will be ladies on the Colne Town Council. I could vote for that myself."*

He was clearly a man ahead of his time.

*Above: Hartley Homes, Colne*

## Top honour in the Primitive Methodist Church

The same year he was awarded the Freedom of Colne William was elected unanimously to the highest position a layman could hold in the Primitive Methodist Church: President of the Conference. He was only the second non-ordained person within a hundred years to be entrusted with this important leadership role.

As President, he chaired meetings with great efficiency, ensuring that the delegates always kept to the point. On one occasion when a matter of £20 was under debate, he remarked humorously, although pointedly, "*I could make the money in the time that you are talking about it.*"

Financial problems were a regular cause of concern to the denomination and because of this many good projects could not go ahead. In one of his addresses, William was uncompromising in pointing out the solution:

*"At present we are held back in our medical missions, our foreign missions, our home missions … for want of money. I am persuaded … that all our financial difficulties would soon disappear … if only every disciple of Jesus Christ willingly consecrated to the Master's service a definite share of his income."*

He explained why this wasn't happening:

*"Primitive Methodists who are now successful men of business tell me … they cannot bring their mind to support religious and philanthropic enterprises with the liberality*

*they should, not because they have not got the money, nor because they do not admit it to be their duty, but because they have not sufficiently developed the disposition to give."*

This was a message that William delivered on many occasions. He had the moral authority to do so because he led by example.

### The Titanic disaster

In 1912 a tragedy occurred that shocked the world and plunged Colne into grief. In the early hours of 15 April, the world's largest liner, the Titanic, sank after hitting an iceberg on its maiden voyage across the Atlantic Ocean. Among the 1,517 dead was a native of Colne, 33-year-old Wallace Hartley. Although not related to Wallace, William, along with the people of Colne, felt a deep sense of personal loss. He was one of us.

Wallace, a devout Christian and an excellent violinist, was the leader of the 8-member-band on the ship. As soon as he realized the Titanic was sinking, he assembled his musicians to play cheerful tunes on deck to calm and comfort the passengers. The band played continuously for two hours until the very end.

*Left: Replica Titanic, Colne*

*Above: Wallace Hartley, Titanic's bandmaster*

When the ship began to tilt for its final descent, Wallace thanked his fellow musicians and released them from duty. As they walked away, he struck up the opening notes of the hymn *Nearer my God to Thee.* They turned back and joined him. Minutes later they were washed away and drowned.

The story of the band's bravery in the face of death inspired newspaper headlines worldwide. *Nearer my God to Thee* became an anthem of courage and hope and symbolised light in the

*Above: Titanic's band*

midst of darkness. It was played at the funerals and memorial services of many of those who had perished.

Ten days after the sinking, Wallace's body – with his violin case strapped to it – was recovered by a search ship together with those of two of his band. He was the only one of the three brought back to England for burial. His funeral on 18 May became the focus of national grief and international attention.

It was held at the Bethel Methodist Church in Colne where he had been a choirboy. Designed to hold 700 people, about a thousand were present. Some 40,000 people – almost double the population of Colne – lined the streets as the cortège, led by several brass bands, made its way through the town. It took more than an hour to reach the cemetery a quarter of a mile away from the chapel.

On 24 May a memorial concert for the band took place at the Royal Albert Hall with seven of the world's leading orchestras combined into one, the largest ever assembled. It was conducted by some of the top conductors of the day including Sir Edward Elgar and Sir Henry Wood. The concert concluded with the singing of *Nearer my God to Thee* with deep emotion by the whole audience.

*Above: Wallace Hartley Memorial, Colne*

Well before Wallace Hartley's funeral, Colne Town Council had decided to launch an appeal for funds to erect a memorial to him. William immediately made a challenge offer which was announced in *The Times*:

> *"Sir W.P.Hartley, who is a native of Colne, has promised to contribute a sum equal to 10 per cent of the total amount subscribed towards the town's memorial to the bandmaster."*

The amount needed was duly raised. William's was the largest donation by a single individual.

### World War 1
Two years after the Titanic tragedy, an even greater catastrophe occupied the thoughts of the nation, the outbreak of the First World

*Above: David Lloyd George statue, London*

War. Almost immediately David Lloyd George, the Chancellor of the Exchequer, formed a small group of the best business minds in the country to advise him on crucial financial matters. William was one of them.

But not even the best business minds in the country escaped the devastating impact of the war. William felt its effects sharply. On the personal level he was overwhelmed with grief when his *"dearly loved grandson"*, Hartley Barkby, a 19-year-old officer with the Royal Field Artillery, was killed on the Somme in 1916.

On the business level things became so bad that at one point he wondered if his company would survive. Sugar was in short supply and its cost escalated. Fruit quantities were greatly reduced because increased acreage was allocated to the growth of essential crops such as wheat for bread. There was also a severe labour shortage due to enlistment in the armed forces.

Despite all this, the public noticed that Hartley's jam maintained its pre-war quality and prices were not raised. William was never tempted to take moral short cuts, stating:

*"We were resolved – I was very firm on it myself – not to make profit out of national necessities."*

However, no amount of external pressure could put a brake on his commitment to supporting worthy causes. He made generous donations to hospitals and to bodies such as the Red Cross and he gave financial support to the families of any of his employees serving in the armed forces. Martha personally delivered envelopes to them containing money.

### Failing health

The strain of the war years took a great toll on William's health. By 1919 he was suffering angina attacks at the slightest exertion. That year he was offered the position of Mayor of Colne but declined on medical advice. In view of his failing health, it was decided it would be sensible to move from his grand house in Lord Street, Southport, the family home of the previous fifteen years, to a more easily managed house in the Birkdale district of the town.

Fortunately William's son-in-law, John Higham, eased his business pressures by helping to run the Aintree works. The London factory was already in his son John's hands. William was able, therefore, to devote more time to his philanthropic work.

### New hospitals for Liverpool and Colne

Before the war, William had planned to fund two new hospitals, a maternity hospital in

*Left: William Hartley's house, Lord Street, Southport*

Liverpool and a larger, much better equipped hospital in Colne to replace the outdated Cottage Hospital. His original intention was to complete the Liverpool hospital in time for his Golden Wedding but the outbreak of war put an abrupt end to his plans. He resolved, however, to resume the Liverpool and the Colne projects after the war.

By 1921 it was possible to pick up where he had left off. That year he donated a site for the Liverpool Maternity Hospital and gave a huge sum of money towards the cost of building it. On 3 September he fulfilled his pre-war promise to Colne when he laid the foundation stone of a new hospital on a site directly next to the Hartley Homes he had built for the aged poor.

It is a measure of William's commitment to the fight against sickness and disease that he was undeterred by the phenomenal rise in post-war building costs. The new Colne hospital – to be named the Hartley Hospital – would now cost four times more to build than before the war. But he would cut no corners. In his address to the 10,000 people present when he laid the

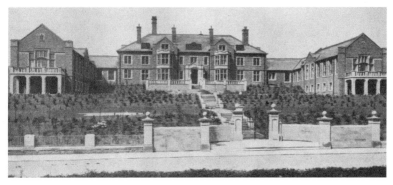

*Above: Hartley Hospital, Colne*

foundation stone, he declared:

*"You can rely upon my promise that everything known to medical science will be provided in it and that nothing will be left undone to make it complete and up-to-date in every particular."*

At the same time, he reaffirmed the close bond he and Martha felt with Colne:

*"My wife and I never forget that we were born in Colne, and in the erection of this hospital we have endeavoured to show in a practical manner our affection for our native town."*

### Death and funeral

William followed the building progress of the Hartley Hospital in Colne with close interest but sadly did not live to see it finished. In 1922, just a year after laying the foundation stone, his health problems caught up with him. When he went to bed on Tuesday 24 October he told his daughter Christiana he felt unwell. Christiana, the only one of his seven daughters not married, was running the household. She checked on him three times during the night and was extremely worried that he seemed to be declining. When he woke in the morning he said he felt much better and intended to visit his works in Aintree. But he didn't get there. As he climbed out of bed he suffered a massive heart attack and died. He was 76.

*Above: William's daughter, Christiana*

44

At the news of his death the flags at Southport Town Hall and Southport Liberal Club were flown at half-mast. His funeral service was held three days later at the Primitive Methodist Chapel in Derby Road, Southport, known locally as 'The Jam Chapel' because William had built it.

After the service William's body was transported by road some 50 miles to Colne for his burial in Trawden Cemetery in the hills above the town to be laid to rest with his parents and his little daughter Martha. The flag at Colne Town Hall was flown at half-mast and as the procession passed through the town to the cemetery all shops were closed and blinds drawn as a mark of respect for a great and much-loved man. Concurrent with the interment in the cemetery a service was held at the Aintree Primitive Methodist Chapel attended by many of William's grateful employees.

His death had made national news and the following Sunday congregations in churches and chapels across the country paused respectfully to reflect on his life and passing.

### The secret of William's success

William's products were widely regarded for their quality, even gracing the table of royalty. And when the renowned Polar explorer Robert Falcon Scott set out on his courageous Antarctic expedition of 1910-13 in an attempt to be the first

*Above: Jam Chapel, Southport*

man to reach the South Pole, he took supplies of Hartley's jam with him. After World War 1 a former serviceman could write that Hartley *"gave the fighting Tommies his very best jams"*. This was also the case during World War 2 as the following company advertisement reveals:

*Below: William's grave, Trawden Cemetery*

*"Hartley's give you their word that they will keep QUALITY UP and PRICES DOWN as long as is humanly possible."* (Their capitalisation).

The advertisement concluded with the slogan: *"HARTLEY'S – "the greatest name in jam-making"*.

It was clearly a claim the company felt able to live up to.

Because Hartley's jam is still appreciated for its quality and taste, many would argue that the slogan remains valid today. No doubt it would have delighted William to know that the tradition he started of giving customers only the best, lives on. But would he like to be remembered for this alone? Was this the sole secret of his success?

Today fame and fortune tend to define a person's worth and William would no doubt be admired for establishing a brand that made him enormously wealthy. But he would instantly have dismissed fame and fortune as the measure of a person's value or as a guarantee of happiness. He made this quite clear:

*"Thank God, happiness is from within, not from without. It is what a man is, and not what a man has."*

He was careful to apply the standard of *"what a man is"* to himself:

*Above: Sir William Hartley*

*"I am much exercised as to whether I am such a disciple of Jesus Christ that my work people, my business friends, my neighbours and my family can constantly see the Spirit of the Master in my actions".*

So what was the secret of success as William saw it? His own words provide a fitting conclusion to his story:

*"My last word must be that we … followers of Jesus Christ, must carry into our life His spirit and teaching, and that whatever we think Jesus Christ would have done, had He been in our place, whether we are employers or employed, whether we are in business or out of business, that we are compelled to do. This is the secret of all true success; the consecration of ourselves and our substance to Him who loved us and laid down His life for us."*

## ACKNOWLEDGEMENTS

The following have given me invaluable help with my research. I am most grateful to them.

Christine Bradley, *Reference & Local Studies Librarian, Colne Library*

Roger Hull, *Research Officer, Record Office, Central Library, Liverpool*

Sue Kauffman, *Libraries Archives, Record Office, Central Library, Liverpool*

Debbie Kershaw, *Finance & HR Administrator, St Mark's Medical Centre,*
      *Southport*

Canon Dr Jon Richardson, *Former Diocesan Director of Education, Liverpool*

Billy Smith, *Archivist, Everton FC Heritage Society, Liverpool*

Darran Ward, *Library Service, Colne Library*

## IMAGES

Amberley Publishing have very kindly given permission to use the following:

William Hartley (p 2)

William aged 19 (p 5)

William with his family (p 10)

Enjoying Hartley's jam (p 13)

A picking room, Aintree factory (p 16)

Sunken floor areas, Aintree factory (p 18)

Unloading a delivery of oranges, Aintree factory (p 20)

Checking oranges for quality, Aintree factory (p 22)

The London Works (p 30)

Kind permission has also been given to use the following:

Graham Murphy – George Mahon, Houlding's fierce opponent (p 24)

Briercliffe Society, Burnley – Cottage Hospital, Colne (p 28)

Englesea Brook Chapel & Museum – Hartley College, Manchester (p 33)